# Welcome to Busy Book 4!

These things are hidden in this book.
Can you find them?
Write the page number in the star.

The Busy Book helps children develop in the following areas of learning...

 **Communication**
Learning to speak together
in English.

 **Leadership**
Learning to build relationships.

 **Discovery**
Building knowledge and awareness
of social responsibility.

 **Critical thinking**
Solving problems and puzzles and
learning thinking skills.

 **Creativity**
Expressing ideas through drawing
and making.

 **Self-management**
Learning to plan ahead to reach goals.

# 1 Who are we?

**Find Sofia's friend.**

*My friend has got...*

*My friend hasn't got...*

blonde hair.

wavy hair.

straight, black hair.

Ben    Martin    John

Lucy    Bella

glasses.

a smile.

a moustache.

*My friend's name is _____.*

## Spot the difference.

### Julian

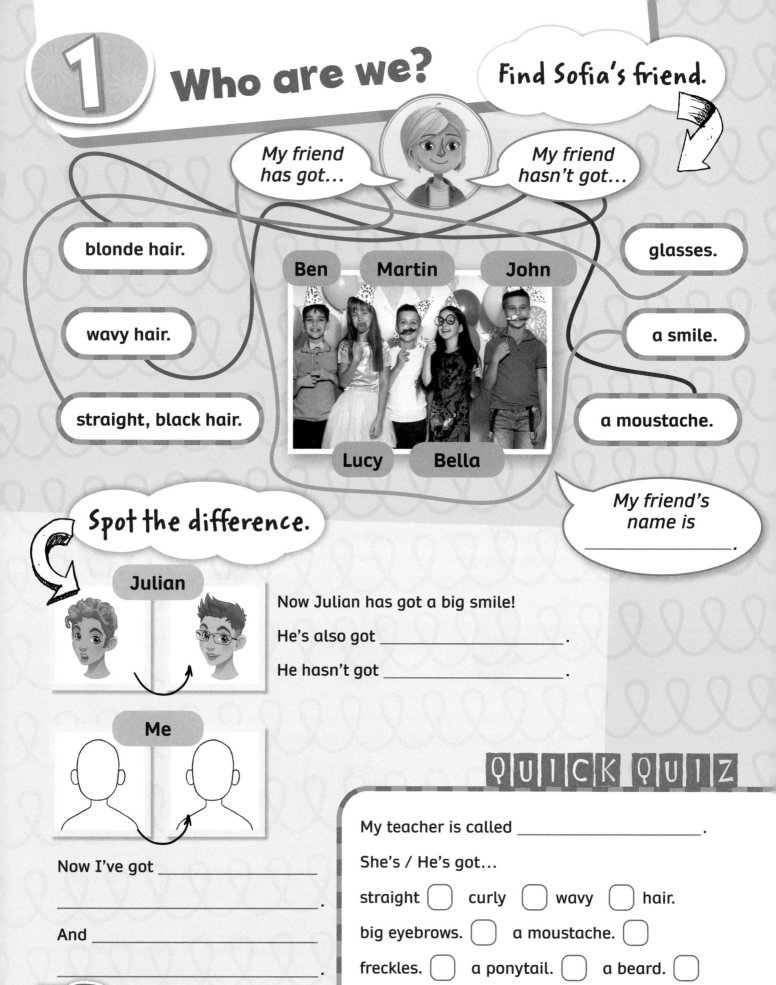

Now Julian has got a big smile!

He's also got _____ .

He hasn't got _____ .

### Me

Now I've got _____
_____ .
And _____
_____ .

## QUICK QUIZ

My teacher is called _____ .

She's / He's got...

straight ☐    curly ☐    wavy ☐    hair.

big eyebrows. ☐    a moustache. ☐

freckles. ☐    a ponytail. ☐    a beard. ☐

# Who's got the necklace?

**Imagine with Hugo**

Read and complete.

## CITY NEWS

### STOLEN NECKLACE!

The police are looking for a special necklace. They've got a letter with some information. "There are a lot of numbers," says Detective Smith, "but we don't understand it!"

a=26, b=25 ➡ y=2, z=1

**WHO'S GOT THE NECKLACE?**

**THE PERSON HAS GOT...**

4 26 5 2 / 19 26 18 9   w _ _ _ / _ _ _ _ r .

13 12 / 25 22 26 9 23   _ _ / _ e _ _ _ .

25 18 20 / 22 26 9 9 18 13 20 8   _ _ _ / _ _ _ _ _ _ _ _ .

26 / 25 9 26 24 22 15 22 7   _ / _ _ _ _ _ _ _ _ .

### Can you help the police?

Use the code. Complete the letter. Who's got the necklace?

_____

_____ has got the necklace.

DAN    JILL    EVA    MIA    BOB

Invent your own code. Write a message to a friend.

| a | b | c | d | e | f | g | h | i | j | k | l | m | n | o | p | q | r | s | t | u | v | w | x | y | z |
|---|---|---|---|---|---|---|---|---|---|---|---|---|---|---|---|---|---|---|---|---|---|---|---|---|---|
|   |   |   |   |   |   |   |   |   |   |   |   |   |   |   |   |   |   |   |   |   |   |   |   |   |   |

3

# Guessing game

Complete and play the 'Who is it?' game.

| | | | |
|---|---|---|---|
| Alex | Lisa | Carla | Charlie |
| Marcus | Juan | Anna | Mei |
| Ben | Kwame | Lucy | Tom |
| Nick | Katie | Asim | Daisy |

Katie has long wavy hair and earrings.

Tom has short straight hair and glasses.

Sorry, I don't understand. Can you say that again, please?

Is it a girl?

Yes.

Has she got long hair?

No, she hasn't.

Is it Lisa?

Yes, it is!

**Tongue twister**

Can you say this quickly five times?
*Clever Colin has got great glasses!*

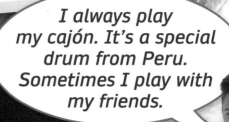

## Explore with Eva

# Our world

**Match the drums to the countries.**

I always play my cajón. It's a special drum from Peru. Sometimes I play with my friends.

We often play our drums in competitions.

Nigeria

Scotland

We never feel sad when we play our drums!

**Explore more**

Find out about more drums from around the world. Draw.

**Find someone who has one of these special things.**

☐ drum  ☐ necklace  ☐ bracelet
☐ earrings  ☐ coin  ☐ blanket

_____'s special thing is a _____.

It's _____

_____.

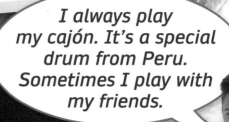

5

# My funny characters

Choose and draw your characters.

| princess | police officer | blonde | green | hair | earrings |
|----------|----------------|--------|-------|------|----------|
| superhero | waiter | straight | pink | eyebrows | a blanket |
| monster | bus driver | curly | yellow | moustache | a necklace |
| spy | doctor | wavy | red | nose | a bracelet |

**Dr Monster**

_____

_____

My characters are called _____ and _____.

_____ has got _____ but hasn't got _____.

_____ has got _____ but hasn't got _____.

My favourite activity in this unit:

_____

My new words:

_____

_____

I will find out more about:

_____

_____

Can you write a story about your characters?

6

# Let's use it again!

**2**

Count the words and colour.

- ☐ boxes
- ☐ cups
- ☐ bowls
- ☐ pots
- ☐ rugs

Use a mirror and match.

sweater

jacket

plate

handbag

shelf

## QUICK QUIZ

Name something you put...

| | |
|---|---|
| on a plate. | _____ |
| in a handbag. | _____ |
| on a shelf. | _____ |
| in a box. | _____ |

# What's in the box?

Read and complete the story.

Millie and Jack are in a dark room in an old, scary house.

"Look at those boxes on that old, metal shelf!" says Jack.

Millie opens the first box. "This is a rubber duck."

Jack opens the second box. "These are plastic cups and glass plates. Nothing special."

Millie opens the third box. Under some brown paper, she finds something very special.

"Look, Jack! Whose are these _____?"

"They're yours now! And mine!" says Jack.

"Excuse me... they're MINE!" says _____!

 Use these ideas or your own.

Draw a picture of the ending of your story.

| metal | rubber | plastic |
| wood | paper | glass |

| coins | necklace |
| photos | paintings |

# Island hop

Take turns to spin the spinner. When you get to an island or go past one, invite your friend.

## You will need:

 a spinner  two counters

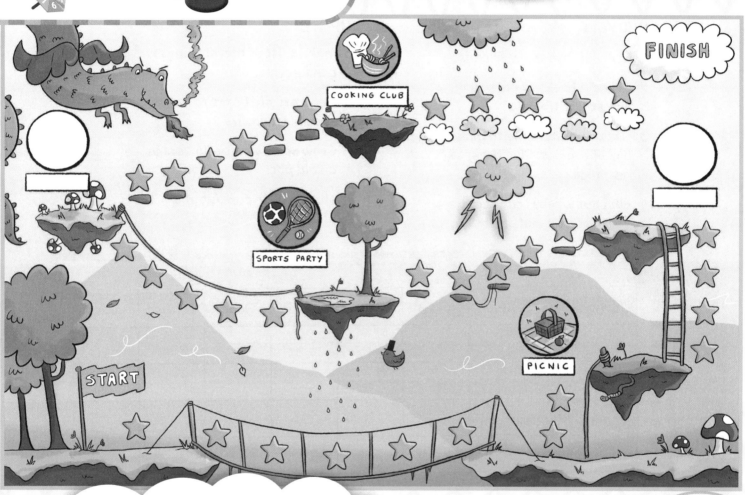

Add your own two islands to the game.

Would you like to come to *a picnic*?

Yes, please. I'd love to!

No, thanks. Sorry, I can't!

Tell me a joke!

What goes up but never comes down?

Your age!

9

# Our world

## What can I do? Tick.

**RECYCLE**

1 Give old toys to my friends. ☐

2 Give old books to my school, hospital or library. ☐

3 Use things at home to make a huge box of cookies. Give them to a neighbour. ☐

4 Find out where I can recycle glass, plastic and paper. ☐

**UPCYCLE**

5 Make a list of metal things I can upcycle. ☐

6 Decorate old boxes to put my special things in. ☐

7 Grow some pretty flowers in an old pot. ☐

8 Make a little cup out of a plastic pot. ☐

| At home, I recycle... | paper | metal | plastic | wood | rubber | glass |
|---|---|---|---|---|---|---|
| always | | | | | | |
| often | | | | | | |
| sometimes | | | | | | |
| never | | | | | | |

### Explore more

**Where can you recycle things in your town or city?**

the recycling centre   the supermarket
the town square   home   school   the community centre

I can recycle _____ at _____.

# My upcycling ideas

Can you find old things in your home to upcycle?

Draw or stick photos.

Use your old things. Design an upcycled gift for a friend.

I can upcycle these rubber boots to make flower pots!

I can upcycle _____

_____

to make

_____.

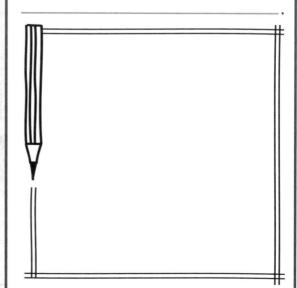

My favourite activity in this unit:

_____

My new words:

_____

_____

I will find out more about:

_____

_____

11

# 3 City of the future

Find and draw the places.

ice rink   shopping centre
funfair   stadium   restaurant
~~art gallery~~   swimming pool

You can go up, down, left or right!

| | | Olga | | Kelly | R ▶ | | |
|---|---|---|---|---|---|---|---|
| I | D | S | K | F | I | A | |
| U | A | T | N | U | N | F | T |
| M | E | R | I |  | R | A | N |
| William ▶ I | C | S | T | A | U | R | Y  ▶ |
| Dan ▶ R | E |  | | | E | L | ▶ |
| Ahmed ▶ A | R | T | G | A | L | L | O |
| I | M | M | I | N | G | P | O |
| W | G | C | E | N | T | R | E ▶ |
| Maria ▶ S | N | I | P | P | O | H | S ◀ Pam |

## Think and write.

🏠 + 🎨 + 🖥 + 🍳 + 🚶‍ = h _ _ _ _

Draw a code for a place in town. Ask a friend to guess.

## QUICK QUIZ

I can see...

special paintings at the _____.

fun rides at the _____.

popular shows at the _____.

amazing footballers at the _____.

Draw the animals.
What do they like doing?

**Hippo**

At the funfair, Hippo likes going on a ride.
"I enjoy it because it's fun!"

At the stadium, Tiger likes watching a match.
"I like watching the footballers run!"

**Tiger**

At the theatre, Lion loves watching a show.
It's something he always enjoys.

**Lion**

Monkey likes going shopping.
He loves looking at all the toys.

**Monkey**

Penguin likes going to a restaurant.
He goes with his friends from the pool.

**Penguin**

And at the museum, they love exhibitions,
they're interesting, fun and cool!

Your turn!

**Draw or stick in a photo.**

I like going _____

because _____.

I also like _____

_____.

# Maze challenge

**Find the gold.**

**START**

## Instructions:

Draw five more gold coins 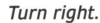 on the board. Play a game with a friend. Tell your friend where to go.

**FINISH**

*Turn left.*

*Turn right.*

*Go straight on.*

*Stop!*

 **Choose your challenge!**

Find all the gold and get to the FINISH in

◯ 5 minutes.  ◯ 2 minutes.  ◯ 30 seconds.

## Riddle

Where am I? The first part sounds like *sun* and the second part sounds like *hair*.

# Our world

Let's do a city tour!

Choose your tour. Tick.

## I like...

| | | | |
|---|---|---|---|
| ▲ new things. ◯ | ● acting. ◯ | ▪ ice cream. ◯ |
| ▪ sports. ◯ | ▲ having a picnic. ◯ | ▲ sharing. ◯ |
| ▪ exciting places. ◯ | ▪ being outside. ◯ | ▲ cute things. ◯ |
| ▲ being with my friends. ◯ | ● old things. ◯ | ▪ playing football. ◯ |
| ▲ pizza. ◯ | ▲ clothes. ◯ | ● painting a picture. ◯ |
| ● learning. ◯ | ● interesting places. ◯ | ● being inside. ◯ |
| ▪ scary things. ◯ | ● being by myself. ◯ | ▪ going on adventures. ◯ |

Which tour is your favourite? Count.

◯ ▪ **Fun outside:** Do you like activities that are exciting, fun and sometimes scary? Let's enjoy going on rides at the funfair or watching a match at the stadium!

◯ ▲ **Food and friends:** Do you like having fun with your friends and sharing new things? Let's enjoy going to restaurants and going shopping at the shopping centre or at the market!

◯ ● **Culture:** Do you like learning, watching things and visiting interesting places? Let's enjoy watching shows at the theatre and going to exhibitions at the museum!

**Explore more**

Think about places in your town or city. Then write.

I like _____ because it's lovely.

I like _____ because it's clean.

I don't like _____ because it's boring.

I don't like _____ because it's dirty.

I like _____ because it's _____.

_____ because it's _____.

# My city break

Create the perfect city day trip for friends or family.

I'm creating a Saturday city trip for

_____.

Show at 7 p.m. every Saturday.

Exhibition open 9 a.m. – 5 p.m. at the weekend.

Ask your friends or family what they like doing before you plan.

Football match on Saturday at 7 p.m.

Open daily 10 a.m. – 8 p.m.

Write and draw or stick photos.

Saturdays 8 a.m. – 1 p.m.

Open 8 a.m. – 8 p.m. at the weekend.

| _____'s city | |
|---|---|
| **Saturday trip!** | |
| **Morning** | |
| | We're going to the _____ because _____ likes _____. |
| **Afternoon** | |
| We're going to the _____ because _____ likes _____. | |
| **Night** | |
| | We're going to the _____ because _____ likes _____. |

My favourite activity in this unit:

_____

My new words:

_____

_____

I will find out more about:

_____

_____

# Food for everyone!

Count the foods to complete the puzzle.

Circle the odd one out.

pasta   lemons
rice   bread

pineapples   grapes
potatoes   apples

milkshake   water
orange juice   beans

## QUICK QUIZ

What's your favourite...

fruit? _____

vegetable? _____

drink? _____

The hidden fruit is: ☐ ☐ ☐ ☐ ☐ ☐

Choose and write. Then draw your funny café, the waiter, chef and the food!

| astronaut | dragon | teacher | monster | inventor |
|---|---|---|---|---|
| happy | scary | huge | cool | special |
| soup | rice | pasta | pizza | honey |
| box | bag | cup | glass | bottle |
| olives | lemons | pineapples | vegetables | potatoes |
| sofa | plate | bicycle | shelf | blanket |
| two | five | twenty | fifty two | one hundred |

## Welcome to the Rainbow Café!

Our chef is a      who can make      dishes for you.

Sit on a      and choose your food. Our      waiter brings all the dishes on a     . There's a lot of with      and     . There's also some      with a lot of      and     . Is there any waste? No, there isn't! Not at our      café!

Come on your birthday and we give you a      of      and           in a      to take home!

Tell your friends and family about your café!

18

# How much is it?

 Ask, remember and answer!

## Instructions:

1 Player 1 looks and remembers the prices.

2 Player 2 hides the picture from Player 1 and chooses a food to talk about.

 How much is it?

**Player 1**

It's £1.50.

**Player 2**

Sugar?

Yes! My turn.

**Tongue twister**

Can you say this quickly five times?

*Sit down now, big brown cow!*

# Our world

*Let's make lunch! I've got...*

a bowl of **beans**

some **bread**

a cup of **rice**

a lot of **carrots**

a box of **tomatoes**

**Spain: paella**

Eva can use
_____.

**UK: a sandwich**

Eva can use
_____.

**Explore more**

What dish can you make from your country using Eva's food? Draw and write.

I can use _____

to make _____.

**Japan: bento box**

Eva can use
_____.

**Mexico: pico de gallo**

Eva can use
_____.

# QUICK QUIZ

To not waste food, I like to...

...make ☐ a smoothie. ☐ a cake. ☐ lemonade. ☐ chips.

...share with friends. ☐ family. ☐ _____

# My pizza menu

Design pizzas for a new restaurant!

## My no-waste list

a bag of _____

a piece of _____

a box of _____

a bottle of _____

a _____ of _____

a _____ of _____

## Pizza menu

**Pizzas**

_____
£_____

_____
£_____

_____
£_____

On my pizza menu, there's...

_____
_____

There aren't any...

_____
_____

Can you make your pizzas at home?

**Drinks**

a glass of

_____
£_____

a cup of

_____
£_____

My favourite activity in this unit:

_____

My new words:

_____
_____

I will find out more about:

_____
_____

 21

# Help our oceans!

**Match and draw.**

1 **snail**  2 **jellyfish**  3 **octopus**

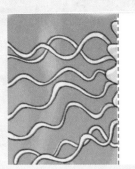 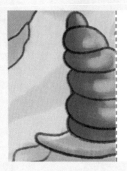 

*What are the animals doing? Tick or cross.*

## CLUES

The sharks are swimming in the cave. They aren't in the plants.

The crab is on the rock. It isn't sitting.

The dolphins are in the sea. They aren't hiding.

The seahorse is in the plants. It isn't playing.

The starfish are sitting. They aren't in the cave.

| | | | | | |
|---|---|---|---|---|---|
| playing | ✘ | | | | |
| swimming | ✔ | ✘ | ✘ | ✘ | ✘ |
| sitting | ✘ | | | | |
| walking | ✘ | | | | |
| hiding | ✘ | | | | |
| in the sea | ✘ | | | | |
| in the plants | ✘ | | | | |
| on the rock | ✘ | | | | |
| on the beach | ✘ | | | | |
| in the cave | ✔ | | | | |

The sharks are __swimming__

in the _____.

The _____ are

_____.

_____

_____.

## QUICK QUIZ

Guess who…

has got a curly shell?  ◯ snail  ◯ seahorse

is a fish?  ◯ whale  ◯ shark

can grow a new arm?  ◯ seal  ◯ starfish

# The big beach clean up

**Read, draw and write.**

Hi! I'm at the beach with my community group. We're having a beach clean up. Our work helps to clean the oceans.

There's a lot of plastic on the beach. It's very dirty! My friends are helping me to pick up rubbish.

Look! There's some plastic, glass, _____ and _____. These pieces of rubbish are damaging our oceans. But we can recycle them.

How many yellow plastic bags of rubbish can you see in the story?

We're making a film to tell people about our beach clean up. Are all my friends looking at the camera? Yes, they are! Smile, everyone!

# 1, 2, 3... What can it be?

Draw the activities.

### Nature trail
Day: Tuesday
Place: the park
Time: four o'clock

### No plastic bag day
Day: Wednesday
Place: the shopping centre
Time: ten o'clock

### Ocean photo exhibition
Day: Wednesday
Place: the shopping centre
Time: one o'clock

### Upcycling day
Day: Thursday
Place: the shopping centre
Time: ten o'clock

### No-waste picnic
Day: Friday
Place: the park
Time: one o'clock

### Octopus dance party
Day: Saturday
Place: the beach
Time: ten o'clock

### Beach clean up
Day: Saturday
Place: the beach
Time: one o'clock

### Tree planting club
Day: Saturday
Place: the park
Time: four o'clock

### Clean water day
Day: Sunday
Place: the beach
Time: ten o'clock

Ask a friend to choose a card.
Ask them 1, 2 or 3 questions.
Then guess.

When is it?

It's on Saturday.

Where is it?

It's at the beach.

What time does it start?

It starts at one o'clock.

Is it the Beach clean up?

Yes!

Tell me a joke!

How do dolphins go to school?

By **octo**bus!

**Explore with Eva**

# Our world

## Our ocean in numbers

Our brilliant oceans have got a problem: plastic pollution.

**What do you know about this topic?**

1. How much of our world is ocean?

☐ 10%    ☐ 50%    ☐ 70%

2. What is the largest ocean animal?

☐ lemon shark    ☐ blue whale    ☐ bottlenose dolphin

3. We use over 500 billion plastic bags a year. That's…

☐ 15    ☐ 150    ☐ 1500    bags for every person on our planet!

4. How many pieces of plastic go into our oceans every day?

☐ 8 million    ☐ 20 million    ☐ 100 million

5. How many baby sea turtles have dangerous plastic inside them?

☐ at least 20%    ☐ at least 60%    ☐ at least 80%

**Explore more**

What rubbish can you find near your home? Can you use it to make art?

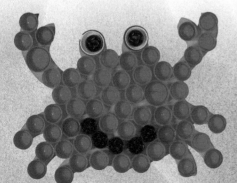

This crab was made with plastic bottle tops.

Draw your Rubbish Art or stick in a photo.

Be safe. Use gloves when you pick up rubbish.

# My ocean tour

Imagine an ocean tour. What can you see? Draw and colour.

Can you talk about your tour for one minute?

How much is your tour?
When does it start?
What are the animals doing?
Is your ocean safe or dangerous?
Is it clean or dirty?

My favourite activity in this unit:

_____

My new words:

_____

_____

I will find out more about:

_____

_____

Write about your picture.

Has it got an important message?

In my ocean tour, there is a

_____ and there are some

_____.

_____

_____

_____

_____

_____

_____

# Let's play together!

## 6

Write and colour.
Then complete and draw.

 ☐☐☐☐☐☐☐☐☐

 ☐☐☐☐☐☐☐☐☐☐☐

 ☐☐☐☐☐☐☐☐☐

 ☐☐☐☐☐☐☐☐☐☐☐

☐☐☐☐☐☐

 ☐☐☐☐☐☐☐☐☐☐☐

 ☐☐☐☐☐☐☐☐

 ☐☐☐☐☐☐☐☐☐☐

Colour red, *blue*
or *orange* for play,
go or *do*.

○

○

☐☐☐☐☐b☐☐☐☐☐☐☐☐

☐☐☐☐☐☐t☐☐☐☐☐☐

## QUICK QUIZ

I like... ✔ but I don't like... ✘

☐ playing volleyball.          ☐ playing badminton.          ☐ going snowboarding.
☐ playing table tennis.        ☐ playing baseball.           ☐ going swimming.
☐ playing hockey.              ☐ doing athletics.            ☐ _____.
☐ playing basketball.          ☐ doing gymnastics.           ☐ _____.

## Imagine with Hugo

# Rabbit and Crab

 **Read the story.**

Rabbit and Crab are going to have a race to the sea.

What are you going to do, Crab? Are you going to run?

No, I'm not. I'm going to fly!

You're going to **fly**?

Yes, I am!

I'm going to win the race!

Rabbit thinks she's the winner. But Crab is flying!

Rabbit is jumping hurdles. She isn't looking behind her. But Crab's got Rabbit's tail.

Where are you, Crab?

Imagine you're an animal. Choose who you want to do a sports activity with. What are you going to do?

| lion | monkey | parrot | tiger | penguin |
| whale | dolphin | mouse | chicken | |

| throw a ball | bounce a ball | |
| hit a ball | run | jump hurdles | fly |

I'm a _____ and I'm going to

_____ , with a _____ !

I'm here! I'm going to go swimming!

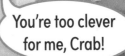

You're too clever for me, Crab!

# Escape the monster!

Ask your friends. Write their names on the track. Complete all ten to escape the monster!

1
2
3
4

1
2
3
4

HOME

## Find someone who is free on...

- ☐ Friday evening.
- ☐ Saturday morning.
- ☐ Sunday afternoon.
- ☐ _____.

## Find someone who wants to...

- ☐ play basketball.
- ☐ watch sport on TV.
- ☐ go swimming.
- ☐ bounce a ball.
- ☐ play a computer game.
- ☐ _____.

Are you free on Friday evening?

No, I'm not.

Yes, I am.

Do you want to go swimming?

No, I don't.

Yes, I do.

## ? Riddle

Where am I?
I can throw, jump and run in the
_____. ?

29

# Our world

Find your unusual sport!

**Are you going to play ball sports?**

Yes → No

**Yes** branch:

Are you going to go to the ocean? → **No**

**Yes** → Can you jump?

Well / Badly

Can you bounce a ball?

Badly / Well

**No** branch:

Do you like animals?

**Yes** → Can you run?

Quickly / Slowly

**No** → Are you going to do an exciting, scary sport?

Yes / No, thank you!

### Pirate Volleyball
Pirates love playing beach volleyball. The winner gets gold coins!

### Octopus Tennis
Playing tennis with an octopus is fun. It's got a lot of arms to hit the ball quickly!

### Space Basketball
Do you want to play basketball on the moon? It's very cool. The ball can bounce high!

### Snail Races
Slowly... slowly... a snail race can take hours, but the snails are very cute!

### Dragon Races
Dragon racing is an exciting sport for brave people. Don't fly badly or you will fall off!

### Sleeping Competition
Just pick up a pillow and close your eyes. Sleep well!

## Explore more

**Think of a sporting hero. Find out three facts about them.**

Name: _____     Sport: _____

FACT 1: _____

FACT 2: _____

FACT 3: _____

# My sports team

Imagine a new sports team!

**Team name:** _____

**Our sport:** _____

**Our players:** ◯ my friends  ◯ superheroes  ◯ animals  ◯ _____

**Player names:** _____

_____

**Our team shirt:**

**Our team badge:**

**My special team**

My new sports team is called

_____.

We are going to

_____

_____

_____

_____.

My favourite activity in this unit:

_____

My new words:

_____

_____

I will find out more about:

_____

_____

31

# Goodbye

## About me

I like this book because...

_____

_____

My favourite activities in this book are...

_____

_____

Something I'm going to remember from this book is...

_____

_____

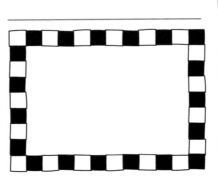

## Rise and Shine Certificate

### You finished Busy Book 4!

### Well done!

Awarded to: _____

Age: _____    Date: _____

Sofia          Hugo          Marco          Eva          Zoe          Socks

Sofia          Hugo          Marco          Eva          Zoe